Basic Skills and Beyond

Long Vowel Sounds

by
Cindy Barden

illustrated by
Shawna Mooney Kawasaki

Activities Support This Learning Outcome

• Students will develop a range of strategies to make meaning from a variety of texts.

Carson-Dellosa Publishing Company, Inc.
Greensboro, North Carolina

Credits:
Project Director: Sherrill B. Flora
Author: Cindy Barden
Inside illustrations: Shawna Mooney Kawasaki
Layout design: Good Neighbor Press
Cover design: Annette Hollister-Papp

 ISBN 0-88724-144-1

Table of Contents

Basic Long Vowels . . .

With the fun activities in this book, your students will listen for the long vowel sounds of **a**, **e**, **i**, **o**, **u**, and **y**. You'll also find these useful skills:

- matching words with pictures
- simple reading
- picture mazes
- unscrambling words
- writing words

Most worksheets need only a pencil and crayons to complete. Spinner games and word games on the Teacher/Parent Pages can be done as a group or one on one.

. . . and Beyond!

Encourage children to take turns making up sentences that use words pictured. Reference the Teacher/Parent Pages to talk about other words with the same vowel sounds.

Let children whose names contain the "vowel sound of the day" have an extra privilege, like being first in line at recess.

Encourage them to bring in objects that match the "vowel sound of the day."

Playing with sounds can be a great learning game. Encourage children to make up tongue twisters and short rhymes.

Let children use all of their senses when they learn phonics:

- Reinforce the sound of long vowel **e** by giving everyone a small piece of cheese. Provide animal crackers in the shape of animals that contain the specific vowel to reinforce learning.
- Let children smell pine when they learn about the long vowel **i** sound.

Children with a strong phonics background become good readers. Get beyond a mere introduction, and give your students a solid long vowel foundation with *Basic Skills and Beyond: Long Vowels.*

A, E, I, O, and U Are Vowels
Sometimes y Is a Vowel

Color the blocks with vowels.

Write the letters that are vowels: ____ ____ ____ ____ ____

Word List: Long Vowel a

This list provides additional words to help students expand their vocabularies. Encourage students to make up rhymes, tongue twisters, poems, or stories with these words.

Abe	flake	make	rail	shape	taste
ace	flame	maid	rain	slate	trace
age	frame	mail	raise	snail	trade
ape	Gail	main	rake	snake	trail
April	gain	male	rate	space	train
ate	gale	mane	rave	spade	vail
baby	game	mate	ray	Spain	vane
bay	gate	may	safe	stage	vase
brace	gave	nail	sail	stain	wade
brain	gay	name	sale	state	wage
brake	glade	pace	same	stay	wave
brave	grain	page	save	table	way
bray	grape	paid	say	tail	whale
cage	gray	pail	shade	tale	
cane	hale	pain	shake	tape	
cape	hail	paint			
cave	hay	pale			
case	jade	pane			
chain	Jake	pave			
crane	James	pay			
crate	Jane	place			
Dale	Jay	plain			
date	Kate	plane			
Dave	Kay	plate			
day	lace	play			
fade	lake	praise			
fail	late	pray			
fake	lay	quail			
fate	made	race			

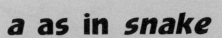

a as in snake

Name _____

A as in *Snake*

Snake has the long vowel **a** sound.

Say the word for each picture.
Listen to the long vowel **a** sound.
Color the pictures.

cave

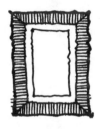

frame

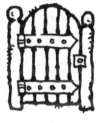

gate

Color the pictures in the frame with the same vowel sound as **snake**.

Name _____

Rainy Day

When the vowels **a** and **i** are together in a word, they often have the long vowel **a** sound.

Pail has the long vowel **a** sound.

Add **ai** to make new words.
Say the new words.

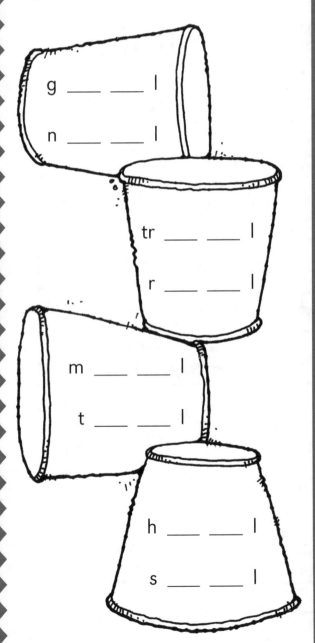

g ___ ___ l

n ___ ___ l

tr ___ ___ l

r ___ ___ l

m ___ ___ l

t ___ ___ l

h ___ ___ l

s ___ ___ l

Rain has the long vowel **a** sound.

Add **ai** to make new words.
Say the new words.

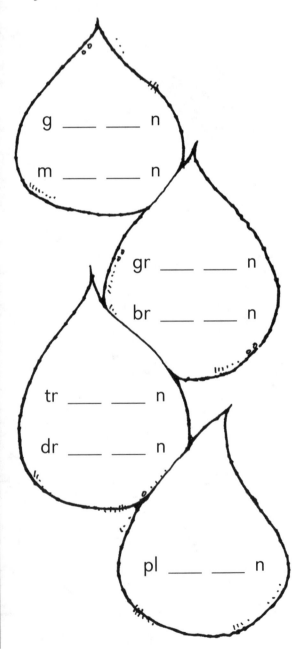

g ___ ___ n

m ___ ___ n

gr ___ ___ n

br ___ ___ n

tr ___ ___ n

dr ___ ___ n

pl ___ ___ n

CD-4708 *Long Vowel Sounds*

Hay Rhymes with Day

When **a** and **y** are together at the end of a word, they have the long vowel **a** sound.

Hay has the long vowel **a** sound.

Fay and Kay like to play in the hay.
Draw Fay and Kay.

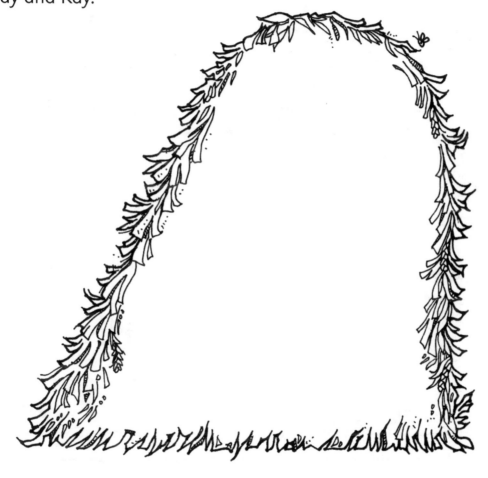

Add **ay** to make words that rhyme with **hay**.

b ___ ___   d ___ ___   j ___ ___   l ___ ___

m ___ ___   n ___ ___   p ___ ___   pl ___ ___

r ___ ___   s ___ ___   st ___ ___   w ___ ___

Name _____

Here Comes the Train

Color the trains if all three words have the long vowel **a** sound.

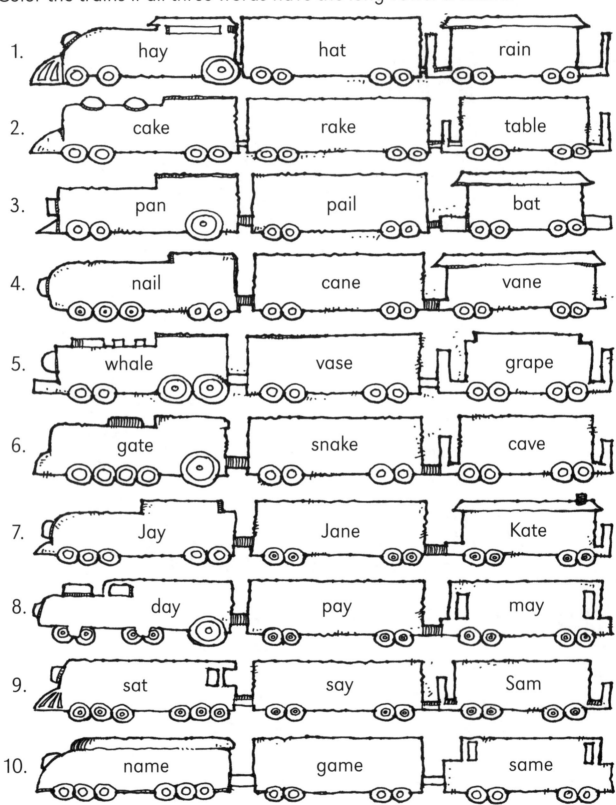

1. hay / hat / rain

2. cake / rake / table

3. pan / pail / bat

4. nail / cane / vane

5. whale / vase / grape

6. gate / snake / cave

7. Jay / Jane / Kate

8. day / pay / may

9. sat / say / Sam

10. name / game / same

Word List: Long Vowels e and i

This list provides additional words to help students expand their vocabularies. Encourage students to make up rhymes, tongue twisters, poems, or stories with these words.

e as in *sheep*

be	green		
beak	greet		
beam	he	peek	
bean	heal	Pete	
beat	heap	read	steel
bee	hear	real	stream
beep	heat	rear	street
beet	heel	reed	sweep
cheap	Jean	sea	sweet
cheep	jeans	seal	tea
clean	jeep	seam	team
cream	key	seat	tease
deal	knee	see	tee
dean	leaf	seed	teen
dear	lean	seek	tepee
deer	leap	seem	three
dream	Lee	she	treat
eager	me	sheep	tree
eagle	meal	sheet	weak
eat	mean	sleek	we
eel	meat	sleet	weed
feel	meek	sneak	week
fear	meet	speak	weep
feet	near	squeak	wheel
gear	neat	speed	year
gleam	peak	steam	

bike	knight	rise
bind	lie	shine
bite	life	shrine
bride	light	side
bright	line	sign
climb	live	sight
dice	mice	size
die	might	slice
dime	Mike	slide
dine	mile	slight
dive	mind	smile
fight	mine	spider
find	nice	spine
fine	night	tide
five	nine	tie
flight	pie	tile
Friday	pile	time
glide	pine	tribe
hide	pipe	vine
hike	price	vise
hive	pride	while
ice	prize	white
idea	quite	wide
item	rice	wife
kind	ride	wine
kite	right	wise
knife	ripe	write

i as in *mice*

CD-4708 *Long Vowel Sounds*

11

Name _____

Green Street

Eel has the long vowel **e** sound.

Say the word for each picture.
Listen for the long vowel **e** sound.
Color the pictures green if they have
the long vowel **e** sound.

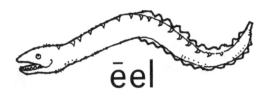

ēel

CD-4708 *Long Vowel Sounds*

Name _____

What Did Jean See?

How many words on this page can you find with a long **e** sound? Circle them. Check your score below.

Jean sees a key in the tree.

Dean reads a book about seas.

Will she eat meat or beans?

What did he see in the stream?

Pete had a dream about sheep.

        17 = You're a pro!
   13–16 = Look again.
less than 12 = Do you need your eyes checked?

Name _____

Meet Me at Three

Circle the words to finish the sentences.
Write the words in the blanks.

1. Pete wore green _____.
                jeans   jam   beans

2. The team will _____ by the tree.
              meet   meal   mean

3. Please clean and _____ the room.
              sheep   sweep   sea

4. Did you _____ the eagle?
              set   seed   see

5. Jean put the bean _____ in the garden.
              weeds   seeds   reeds

6. Would you like baked _____ with your meal?
              beans   bells   bees

7. Will you meet _____ at three o'clock?
              he   me   she

8. Lee had three _____.
              sheep   knees   neat

Name _____

All Mixed Up

Unscramble the letters. Write the words. Color the pictures.

1. erde _____   2. rea _____

3. ele _____   4. ebe _____

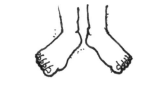

5. etfe _____   6. eta _____

7. erte _____   8. sael _____

9. flea _____   10. desse _____

11. sanbe _____   12. phsee _____

       CD-4708 *Long Vowel Sounds*

Spinner Game

Glue the circle and spinner to heavy cardboard and cut out. Using a hole punch, make a large hole in the spinner.

Attach spinner to center of circle with a brass brad.

Provide game counters, like plastic chips or a bowl of animal crackers.

Children take turns spinning the arrow and naming a word that rhymes. Children receive a game counter or animal cracker for each correct answer.

The wheel sections contain the words: bee, ate, sail, lake, cave, seed, cane, race, feet, eel, bean, eat, ape, game, read, sheep, day, seal.

Name _____

Would You Like a Slice of Pie?

Five has the long vowel **i** sound.

Say the word for each picture.
Listen to the long vowel **i** sound.
Trace the words.

 fīve

bike   bride   knife

dice   nine   tie

pie   dime   vine

knight   hive   smile

CD-4708 *Long Vowel Sounds*

Name _____

Find the Kite

Help the mice find their kite.
Trace a path with pictures that have the same long vowel **i** sound
as **five**.
Color the pictures.

Name _____

A Bike for Mike

Follow the directions.

Draw a bike tor Mike.

Draw a hive for the bees.

Draw a smile on the spider.

Draw a knife for the bride
to cut the cake.

Draw a prize for the knight.

Draw stripes on the kite.

Color nine ties.

Name _____

Rhyme Time

Follow the word pattern. Write words that rhyme.
Say the new words.

mile

p _____
f _____
sm _____

five

h _____
d _____
l _____

nice

r _____
d _____
m _____
sp _____
sl _____

ride

h _____
s _____
w _____
br _____
pr _____

Mike

l _____
b _____
h _____
d _____

night

s _____
br _____
fl _____
l _____

line

f _____
d _____
v _____
p _____
n _____
sh _____
sp _____

Name _____

Red Kites, Green Kites

Say the word for each picture.
Color the kite green if the word has the long vowel **e** sound.
Color the kite red if the word has the long vowel **i** sound.

Make New Words

Copy this page on heavy paper or light cardboard.

Cut out the word strips and letter boxes.

Have children take turns placing the consonants at the beginning of each word strip to determine if that combination makes a new word.

Children who are ready for the challenge can combine two consonants to make blends at the beginning of words.

ike	ee
ice	ear
ine	eat

b	r	d	f
m	h	n	s

Name _____

Missing Vowels

Write the missing vowels for each word.

1. b ___ ___

2. w h ___ l e

3. b ___ k e

4. h ___ y

5. ___ ___ l

6. g r ___ p e s

7. n ___ n e

8. f ___ v e

9. r ___ k e

10. s n ___ k e

11. s ___ ___ d s

12. c ___ k e

13. v ___ n e

14. t r ___ ___

15. t h r ___ ___

CD-4708 *Long Vowel Sounds*

Name _____

Let's Review

Write the words in the group where they belong.

beans	bee	cake	cheese	eagle	eel
five	grapes	Jake	Jay	Jean	Kate
mice	Mike	nine	Pete	pie	seal
three	sheep	snake	spider	whale	

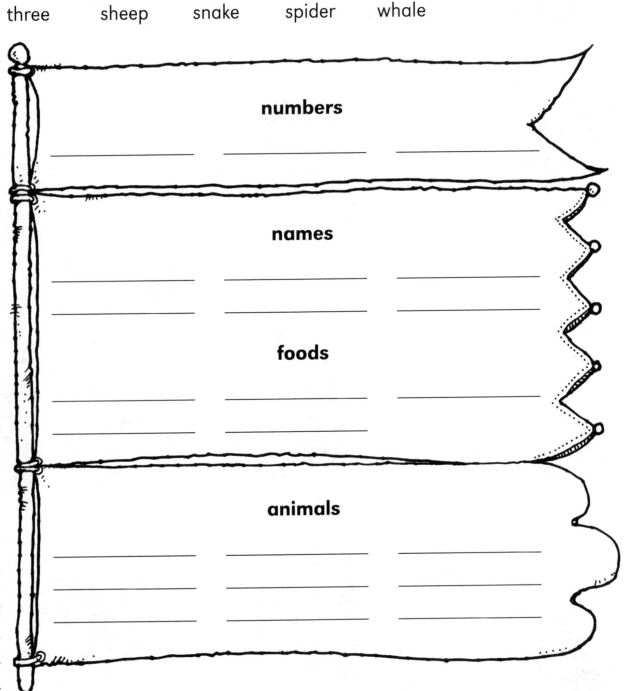

numbers

_____ _____ _____

names

_____ _____ _____

_____ _____ _____

foods

_____ _____ _____

animals

_____ _____ _____

_____ _____ _____

Word List: Long Vowels o and u

This list provides additional words to help students expand their vocabularies. Encourage students to make up rhymes, tongue twisters, poems, or stories with these words.

o as in *bone*

blow	dote	hose	ocean	rose	spoke
boat	float	Joan	Ohio	rote	stone
bone	flow	Joe	open	row	telephone
bow	foal	load	over	scope	throat
bowl	foam	loan	poem	shone	throne
close	go	lone	poet	show	toad
clothes	glow	moan	pole	slope	toe
coal	goal	moat	pose	slow	told
coat	goat	mole	quote	snow	tone
comb	grow	mow	roam	so	tote
cone	hoe	no	role	soak	vole
croak	hole	nose	Rome	soap	vote
crow	home	note	roll	sole	whole
dole	hone	oboe	rope	smoke	zone

blue	flu	June	suit	tuna
Bruce	flute	Lucy	Tuesday	tune
clue	fruit	Luke	true	use
cube	fuse	lute	tuba	
cue	glue	mule	tube	
cute	huge	prune		
due	Jude	rule		
duke	Judy	ruler		
dune	July	Sue		

u as in *mule*

CD-4708 *Long Vowel Sounds*

Name _____

Joe Crow

Crow has the long vowel **o** sound.

crōw

Say the word for each picture.
Listen for the long vowel **o** sound.
Color the pictures with the long vowel **o** sound.

      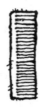      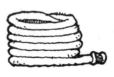

throne   mop   comb   goat   hose

rose   clock   snow   hoe   mole

    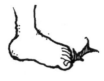         

nose   toe   doll   soap   boat

Name _____

A Goat on the Throne?

Write the words to name the pictures.

Color the pictures.

boat	bowl	comb	cone	crow
goat	mole	rose	throne	toad

CD-4708 *Long Vowel Sounds*

Name _____

Help Toad Go Home

Help the toad find a path across the stones to his home. Trace a path with pictures that have the long vowel **o** sound. Color the pictures.

Name _____

At Crow Lake

Add **a** or **o** to complete the words.
Read the sentences.
Circle YES or NO.
Color the picture.

1. Does K ____ te have a r ____ ke?   YES   NO

2. Is the g ____ at in the b ____ at?   YES   NO

3. Does the g ____ at wear a c ____ at?   YES   NO

4. Is the sn ____ ke in the l ____ ke?   YES   NO

5. Is the wh ____ le in the p ____ il?   YES   NO

6. Does J ____ ke have a c ____ ke?   YES   NO

7. Does K ____ te have sk ____ tes?   YES   NO

8. Does the g ____ at have a r ____ se?   YES   NO

9. Are they at Sn ____ ke L ____ ke?   YES   NO

Name _____

Boat Rhymes with Coat

Color the two pictures in each row that rhyme.

1.

2.

3.

4.

5.

6.

7.

Name _____

Circle the Words

Circle the word for each picture.
Color the pictures.

1. beat
   boat
   beet

2. bike
   bake
   beak

3. dance
   dice
   duck

4. cute
   Kate
   kite

5. rose
   rise
   raise

6. hive
   have
   hum

7. got
   goat
   gate

8. nuts
   none
   nine

9. live
   hive
   five

10. bone
    cone
    tone

11. rope
    ripe
    rap

12. won
    snow
    now

13. pin
    pie
    pay

14. too
    top
    toes

CD-4708 *Long Vowel Sounds*

Teacher/Parent Page
Spinner Game

Glue the circle and spinner to heavy cardboard and cut out. Using a hole punch, make a large hole in the spinner.

Attach spinner to center of circle with a brass brad.

Provide game counters, like plastic chips or a bowl of animal crackers.

Children take turns spinning the arrow and naming a word that rhymes. Children receive a game counter or animal cracker for each correct answer.

Name _____

Home, Sweet Home

Draw lines from the animals to their homes.

Color the pictures.

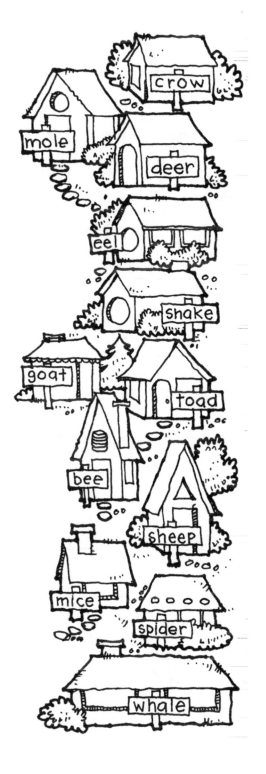

Name _____

Jake Can Bake

Write the words in order to make sentences.

cake   bake   can   a   Jake

_____

- -

_____

meat   Jean   lean   eats

_____

- -

_____

mice   Nine   bikes   ride

_____

- -

_____

crow   old   An   the   mowed   row

_____

- -

_____

to   used   fix   flute   glue   her   Judy

_____

- -

_____

          CD-4708 *Long Vowel Sounds*

Name _____

Cubes of U's

Cube has the long vowel **u** sound.

Say the word for each picture.
Listen for the long vowel **u** sound.
Color the cubes blue if the pictures have the long vowel **u** sound.

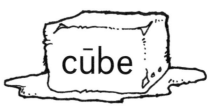

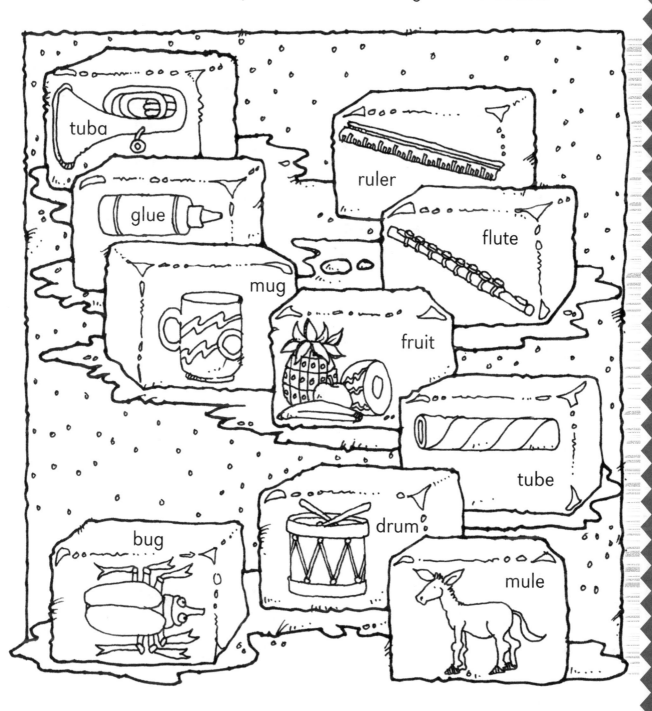

Name _____

Tunes in June

Read the story.

Circle the words with the long vowel **u** sound.

Write the words on the lines.

Bruce can play a flute.

Luke can play a huge tuba.

Sue can play the lute.

Bruce, Luke, and Sue play tunes.

They play tunes on Tuesday.

Judy and Jude like the tunes.

They dance on the dune in June.

Words with long vowel **u** sound.

_____   _____   _____

_____   _____   _____

_____   _____   _____

_____   _____   _____

_____   _____   _____

_____   _____   _____

Draw Judy and Jude as they dance on the dune.

Use the Clues

Read the clues.
Write the answers.

blue	flute	fruit	glue
Judy	July	lute	mule
suit	Tuesday	tuba	tuna

1. I am a day of the week: _____

2. I am a month: _____

3. I am an animal that walks: _____

4. I am a fish: _____

5. I am sticky: _____

6. You can wear me: _____

7. I am a color: _____

8. I am a girl's name: _____

9. You can eat me: _____

10. We can make music: _____

_____

Name _____

Tuba Tunes

Circle the words to finish the sentences.
Write the words on the lines.
Color the pictures.

1. Judy has a _____.
   flute   tuba   lute

2. Bruce wore a blue _____.
   tuba   suit   glue

3. Sue used a _____ of paint.
   tuba   tube   glue

4. Kate _____ to the game.
   come   came   comb

5. The _____ ate fruit.
   mule   mole   mile

6. A _____ is a fish.
   tuba   tube   tuna

7. Jake saw a _____.
   snake   snow   blue

Name _____

Music Makers

Write the words in the group where they belong.

beans	bee	blue	cream	deer	eel
flute	fruit	green	jeans	Judy	July
June	Lucy	Luke	lute	meat	mule
prunes	suit	tuba	tuna		

Colors _____ _____

Clothes _____ _____

Months _____ _____

Music Makers _____ _____

_____ _____

Foods _____ _____

_____ _____

_____ _____

Animals _____ _____

_____ _____

Names _____ _____

_____ _____

Name _____

Mixed-Up Letters

Unscramble the letters. Write the words. Color the pictures.

idce	tsiu	kibe
1. _____	2. _____	3. _____

tfule	eip	buat
4. _____	5. _____	6. _____

vhie	vein	lume
7. _____	8. _____	9. _____

luge	bute	mdei
10. _____	11. _____	12. _____

40

Word List: Y as a Vowel

The letter **y** is often confusing to young learners. Sometimes it is a consonant. Sometimes it is a vowel.

Y is always a vowel if there are no other vowels in the word or syllable of a word.

Y as a vowel can have the sound of long vowel **e** or long vowel **i**.

Y as a Vowel
Sound of long e

Amy	dolly	marry
Andy	empty	Mary
baby	fizzy	merry
Barney	frosty	Molly
Barry	funny	mommy
belly	fuzzy	party
berry	Gary	penny
Betty	Harry	plenty
Billy	Henry	Polly
Bobby	holly	pony
body	ivy	Randy
buddy	Jerry	rocky
buggy	Jimmy	ruby
bunny	Joey	Sandy
bushy	Johnny	Shelly
busy	Judy	sunny
candy	jury	Terry
cherry	kitty	Tony
Cindy	Larry	twenty
city	lucky	very
cozy	Lucy	windy
daddy	many	

Y as a Vowel
Sound of long i

by
cry
dry
fly
fry
July
my
shy
sky
sly
spy
try
why

CD-4708 *Long Vowel Sounds*

Name _____

Y Can Be Tricky

Y as a vowel can have the long vowel **e** or long vowel **i** sound.
Add **y** to make new words.
Say the word.

Listen to the sound at the **end** of the word. If the **y** has the long vowel
e sound, color the cherry green.

If the **y** has the long vowel **i** sound, color the cherry red.

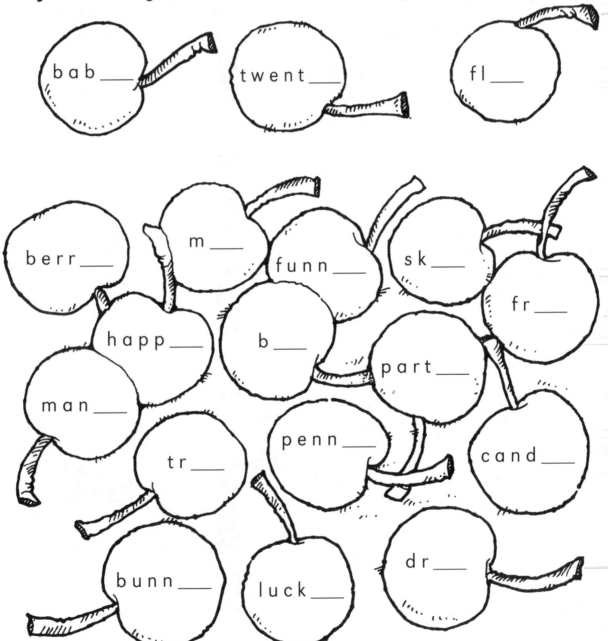

b a b ___   t w e n t ___   f l ___

b e r r ___   m ___   f u n n ___   s k ___   f r ___

h a p p ___   b ___   p a r t ___

m a n ___   t r ___   p e n n ___   c a n d ___

b u n n ___   l u c k ___   d r ___

CD-4708 *Long Vowel Sounds*

Teacher/Parent Page
Spinner Game

Glue the circle and spinner to heavy cardboard and cut out. Using a hole pnch, make a large hole in the spinner.

Attach spinner to center of circle with a brass brad.

Provide game counters, like plastic chips or a bowl of animal crackers.

Children take turns spinning the arrow and naming a word that rhymes. Children receive a game counter or animal cracker for each correct answer.

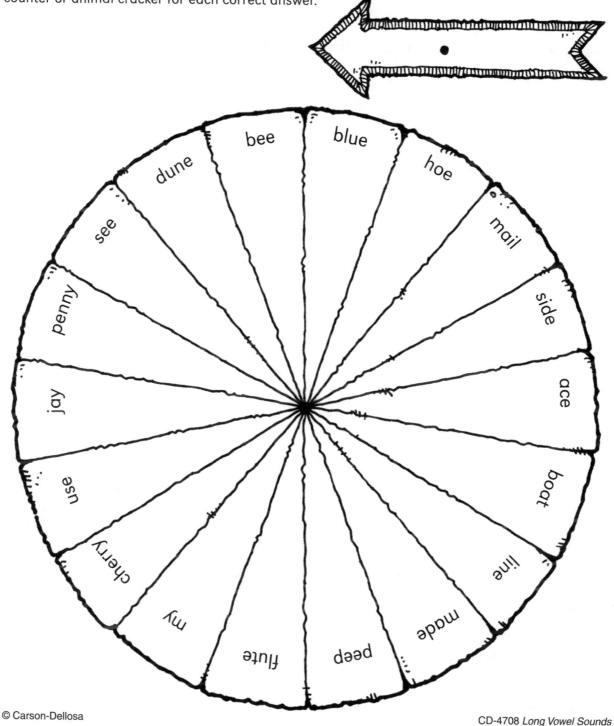

Make New Words

Give each long vowel sound a turn between the two consonants sounds.
What words do you hear?
Circle them.

1. b _____ k

   bake   beak   bike   boke   buke

2. t _____ m

   tame   team   time   tome   tomb

3. m _____ l

   mail   meal   mile   mole   mule

4. m _____ n

   main   mean   mine   moan   moon

5. l _____ n

   lane   lean   line   loan   loon

6. f _____ l

   fail   feel   file   foal   fuel

Name _____

Test: Long Vowels

Circle the correct word for each picture.
Color the pictures.

1. boat / bat / bait	2. bane / bone / brine
3. ruse / rise / rose	4. mole / mule / mile
5. mole / mule / mile	6. flute / flat / flit
7. haze / his / hose	8. dame / dime / dome
9. be / bee / by	10. jeans / Jane / June
11. bake / beak / bike	12. kite / Kate / kitten
13. have / hive / hay	14. tea / eat / ate

Name _____

Test: Y as in *Penny* or *Fly*?

Say the words.
If the **y** has the long vowel **e** sound, write it under the **penny**.
If the **y** has the long vowel **i** sound, write it under the **fly**.

any	baby	by	cry
dry	fry	fuzzy	happy
kitty	jelly	my	silly
sky	spy	try	very

_____

_____

_____

_____

_____

_____

Answer Key

A as in *Snake*, page 7
table, cane, whale, grapes, vane, vase, rake

Here Comes the Train, page 10
trains to color: 2, 4, 5, 6, 7, 8, 10

Green Street, page 12
leaf, tree, cheese, eagle, knee, seeds, three, tea

What Did Jean See?, page 13
Jean, sees, key, tree, Dean, reads, seas, she, eat, meat, beans, he, see, stream, Pete, dream, sheep

Meet Me at Three, page 14
1. jeans
2. meet
3. sweep
4. see
5. seeds
6. beans
7. me
8. sheep

All Mixed Up, page 15
1. deer
2. ear
3. eel
4. bee
5. feet
6. tea
7. tree
8. seal
9. leaf
10. seeds
11. beans
12. sheep

Find the Kite, page 18

Red Kites, Green Kites, page 21
green kites: sheep, seal, three, tree, knee, eagle, tea
red kites: bike, hive, pie, tie, die, nine, dime, five

Missing Vowels, page 23
1. bee
2. whale
3. bike
4. hay
5. eel
6. grapes
7. nine
8. five
9. rake
10. snake
11. seeds
12. cake
13. vine
14. tree
15. three

Let's Review, page 24
numbers: five, three, nine
names: Mike, Jake, Jay, Pete, Jean, Kate
foods: beans, grapes, cake, cheese, pie
animals: mice, bee, sheep, snake, spider, eagle, whale, eel, seal

Joe Crow, page 26
throne, comb, goat, hose, rose, snow, hoe, mole, nose, toe, soap, boat

Help Toad Go Home, page 28

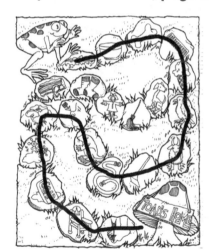

At Crow Lake, page 29
1. a, NO
2. o, YES
3. o, YES
4. a, NO
5. a, NO
6. a, NO
7. a, YES
8. o, NO
9. a, NO

Boat Rhymes with Coat, page 30
1. boat and coat
2. bone and cone
3. ear and deer
4. crow and snow
5. rose and hose
6. knee and bee
7. nose and toes
8. three and tree

Answer Key

Circle the Words, page 31

1. boat
2. bike
3. dice
4. kite
5. rose
6. hive
7. goat
8. nine
9. five
10. bone
11. rope
12. snow
13. pie
14. toes

Jake Can Bake, page 34

1. Jake can bake a cake.
2. Jean eats lean meat.
3. Nine mice ride bikes.
4. An old crow mowed the row.
5. Judy used glue to fix her flute.

Cubes of U's, page 35

tuba, ruler, flute, glue, fruit, tube, mule

Tunes in June, page 36

words with long u: Bruce, flute, Luke, huge, tuba, Sue, lute, Bruce, Luke, Sue, tunes, Tuesday, Judy, Jude, dune, June

Use the Clues, page 37

1. Tuesday
2. July
3. mule
4. tuna
5. glue
6. suit
7. blue
8. Judy
9. fruit
10. flute, lute, and tuba

Tuba Tunes, page 38

1. flute
2. suit
3. tube
4. came
5. mule
6. tuna
7. snake

Music Makers, page 39

Colors: blue, green
Clothes: suit, jeans
Months: July, June
Music Makers: lute, tuba, flute
Foods: beans, prunes, fruit, cream, meat (tuna)
Names: Lucy, Luke, Judy (June)
Animals: bee, tuna, deer, eel, mule

Mixed-Up Letters, page 40

1. dice
2. suit
3. bike
4. flute
5. pie
6. tuba
7. hive
8. vine
9. mule
10. glue
11. tube
12. dime

Y Can Be Tricky, page 42

green: baby, twenty, berry, funny, happy, party, many, penny, candy, bunny, lucky

red: fly, my, sky, fry, by, try, dry

Make New Words, page 44

1. bake, beak, bike
2. tame, team, time, tomb
3. mail, meal, mile, mole, mule
4. main, mean, mine, moan, moon
5. lane, lean, line, loan, loon
6. fail, feel, file, foal, fuel

Test: Circle the Words, page 45

1. boat
2. bone
3. rose
4. mole
5. mule
6. flute
7. hose
8. dime
9. bee
10. jeans
11. bike
12. kite
13. hive
14. tea

Test: Y as in Penny or Fly?, page 46

y as in penny: any, baby, fuzzy, happy, kitty, jelly, silly, very

y as in fly: by, cry, dry, fry, my, sky, spy, try